# MORGAN'S MIND

## Overcoming Attention Deficit Disorder

by

Frankie Perry

**Gotham Books**
30 N Gould St.
Ste. 20820, Sheridan, WY 82801
https://gothambooksinc.com/

Phone: 1 (307) 464-7800

© 2022 Frankie Perry. All rights reserved.

No part of this book may be reproduced, stored in a retrieval system, or transmitted by any means without the written permission of the author.

Published by Gotham Books (September 25, 2022)

ISBN: 979-8-88775-074-3 (sc)
ISBN: 979-8-88775-075-0 (e)

Because of the dynamic nature of the Internet, any web addresses or links contained in this book may have changed since publication and may no longer be valid.

The views expressed in this work are solely those of the author and do not necessarily reflect the views of the publisher, and the publisher hereby disclaims any responsibility for them.

This book is dedicated to:

My granddaughter, I love you more than your mind could ever imagine.

Stephanie from Yamacraw, you ARE enough.

It was literally the very first day of school
I was hopeful fourth grade would turn out cool
No longer in the wing with Pre-K thru third
I was soooo excited it was beyond absurd!
Ms. Cooper is our teacher, she's really nice
"Let's introduce ourselves to break the ice"

"Good idea, Ms. Cooper, I love that game"
That's when I announced Morgan's my name
"We have an Uncle Morgan in Memphis, Tennessee"
I heard from a boy who was laughing at me
"So, YOU are a girl who's named after a dude!"
Said that same boy who was being quite rude

I felt really bad having a name for a boy
But Ms. Cooper quickly restored my joy
"Morgan is a name fit for a King or a Queen
So, it fits our princess so regal and pristine."
Her compliment actually made me feel good
Exactly the way a real princess should
I started daydreaming about faraway places
Castles with chandeliers and fancy glass vases

Once back down to earth, I did a double take
This pair was so exact it was impossible to fake
I know it can be very impolite to stare
But when looking at that boy there
were two of him there
I was working very hard on my concentration
But this was no figment of my imagination
"Joseph and Jacob" one of the J pair said
"Jacob and Joseph" said a boy with the same head

"I love it" said Ms. Cooper as she
smiled and grinned
"I am so excited to teach identical twins
You guys, I am a twin, it's my sister and me
We would do the same thing, we'd never agree
Kia and Aneya is what I would always say
But my twin, Neya, flipped it the other way."
Our mother, Mary Frances would say
"girls don't start
The two of you girls are equal in my heart."
"So, J & J here's what we're all gonna do
Recognize you as individuals, not clump you as two."

My bestie pooh is in my class, Ericka Jestine
We all love her eyes, they're bright emerald green
She decorates her wheelchair with lots of flair
And reminds me to focus if, in space, I do stare
Because she's my bestie she understands me
She totally gets my struggle with A D D
Attention Deficit Disorder or ADD for short
It causes my focus to get all out of sorts
No offense to my teachers, I get easily bored
Granny says my mind just hears a different chord
She's a strong advocate on behalf of my education
Knowing that the wrong approach creates frustration

On with the intros, it was now Katrina Otis' turn
I was getting bored at this point, anxious to learn
Then my overactive mind wandered once again
As our class just reached introduction number 10
I was fidgeting a little while randomly thinking
How ships stay afloat instead of always sinking
I realized I wasn't in focus when I heard Azhu
And my response was "May GOD bless you!"
"I'm not sneezing, no allergies, not even a cold
My name is Azhu Nguyen" he said it really bold
I said "well tune up your flute while
I sit at the organ
Cause I am a girl stuck with a name like Morgan!"

Mirhonda and Alonda Earnest were not at all kin
I thought for a second there was another set of twins
But there was another set just not as easy to tell
One was a he, the other a she, Mykell and Michelle
Gino was from Italy. Sonia from El Salvador
There was a boy in the back I hadn't seen before
You see we live in Savannah near a military base
So occasionally we come across an unfamiliar face
This boy stood up and said "I'm Demetraurias"
Sam forgot her manners asking "Are you serious?"

Ms. Cooper came to the defense of my 'boyish' name
For the new kid in town, she did the very same
"Parents have a right to name their new additions
Based on heritage, preference or even traditions
Never ever make a child feel the slightest rejection
Over a given name that was their parents' selection."
Yet I'm thinking, Kia Cooper, if I was permitted to say
Sounds like the cars in my Granny's driveway
"Well are you from Africa?" asked curious Leroy Glen
"No" D answered, "I'm from Detroit, Michigan"
It reminded me of the Detroit lions and my kitty at home
There are simple triggers that make my thoughts roam

At least I'm not alone because just like I do
The kids at my therapy sessions have ADD too
Dr. Pat helps us chunk tasks making them easier to handle
Just as easy as blowing out a birthday cake candle
My parents don't want me to take any pills
Instead, I use strategies to improve my listening skills
They are very proactive when it comes to my needs
Using apps, lists, lighting, or even anxiety beads

But if I did have medication, still, I just bet
It couldn't stop me from thinking of Aunt Jeannette
She bakes a pound cake that makes me scream
Cousin Travis and I eat it with vanilla ice cream
Which is a rare occasion (me enjoying cake)
Because I must carefully watch my sugar intake

The memory of sweets sent me to the 5th dimension
Then Ericka Jestine said "Pssst….Morgan, listen!"
Ms. Cooper said "let's all give John a big hand
His father Gerald James is serving in Afghanistan."
So, we clapped and clapped till our hands were sore
I hoped that was the end but nope there was more
There was Tina, Tony, Stacy, Dot and Lynda Lee
Had we been there for hours or was it just me?

Nevaeh told us her name was heaven in reverse
Yet I took more interest in her bedazzled purse
Blinged out purses are thought-provoking
Was that twin a meanie or only joking?
Near the end we arrived at kid twenty-seven
She said "I'm Angel, but I'm not from heaven"
Ms. Cooper said we were all from a glorious place
As she introduced us to gorgeous Hope-Grace
Well, we finally made it to the very last child
Demetria Denise said "hey" with a smile

"Well students, just as we shared a variety of names
As your teacher I know you don't all learn the same,
That's why I am extremely proud of my reputation
For reaching all learners through differentiation".
Ericka in her wheelchair and me with my busy mind
I was confident that this school year we'd both be fine.
For once I felt as if we both belonged
And not as if our presence was wrong

Ms. Cooper embraced us with such great cheer
She was looking forward to an amazing year
"Embody your names and everything that you are,
You are uniquely a version of a future superstar
Whatever your attributes, be you a boy or a girl,
My job is to guide you to contribute to the world".
So that was our welcome to Ms. Cooper's fourth grade
Ericka and Morgan together, yep, we got this made!

www.ingramcontent.com/pod-product-compliance
Lightning Source LLC
LaVergne TN
LVHW070536070526
838199LV00075B/6796